Joan of Arc

Joan of Arc

BY JOHANNA JOHNSTON

ILLUSTRATED BY W. T. MARS

DOUBLEDAY & COMPANY, INC.

GARDEN CITY, NEW YORK

1961

Contents

*All the chapter headings in this book
are Joan's own words,
taken from the testimony
at her trial.*

*Almost all of the conversations in this book
are the people's actual speeches
as reported in contemporary documents.*

"Because it pleased God
to choose a simple maid . . ."

SHE WAS JUST ABOUT THE MOST ASTONISHING GIRL WHO EVER LIVED. She was so young—and so alone—and she accomplished such fantastic things.

Five hundred years ago and more, she came out of nowhere to stir the people of France to new life. She inspired them, united them, and frightened some of them so badly they put her on trial for her life as a witch.

The only person who stayed completely unsurprised through it all was the girl herself, Joan, whom men called Joan the Maid, or Joan of Arc.

Over and over, she explained how she had been able to do what she did. And she could not see why her explanation was strange or frightening.

She had almost forgotten that once, long before, she had been frightened herself, when the everyday pattern of her little-girl life had suddenly been broken.

The pattern had been so simple in the beginning.

She lived with her parents, and her brothers and her sister, in an old, low-ceilinged, gray stone house, very much like all the other low gray houses in the village where she was born, a little river town called Domremy, far on the eastern border of France.

She looked like any healthy little country girl. She was sturdy, with black hair and sun-tanned skin. If there was anything at all special about her looks, it might have been her eyes, which were large and dark and widely set. She had a way of looking at people too, which was oddly compelling.

"Come!" she would say to her sister, or big brothers, when she was very little and there was something that interested or bothered her. And Catherine, or Jacques or Jean would leave what she or he was doing and follow the little girl, despite the foolishness of it.

Of course a small girl in any family is apt to have that effect. But Joan's wide, dark gaze seemed to keep its magic even as she grew older.

She had her tasks, as everyone did. As soon as she was old enough, her mother taught her how to sew and spin. And sometimes, like the other children, she had to take her turn watching the cattle and sheep as they grazed in the fields beyond the village.

7

What she herself liked best of all was going to church. But this did not mark her as anyone very special in those days either. For everyone, then, faith was the air one breathed and church was the chief part of life. Morning, noon, and night, the bells in the church tower rang for prayers, and Joan loved the sweet clanging of those bells.

So there she was, a quiet, busy little girl, living at the very eastern edge of France at the beginning of the fifteenth century. And what else was there to make her different from millions of other little girls, before or since?

There was, of course, the war. That was part of Joan's life too.

It was a war with England, actually, but it had been going on so long, almost seventy-five years, off and on, and there had been so many quarrels within quarrels during the course of it, that Frenchmen were fighting Frenchmen in some places as well.

Domremy was far from the coast where the fiercest battles with the English took place, but it had its share of troubles.

Joan was only eight, and just learning to sew a straight seam, when suddenly, one day, the bells in the church tower set up a wild and frightening clamor.

Joan dropped her sewing and looked wide-eyed toward her mother. But Isabelle, her arms floury to the elbow from the bread she was kneading, had no answer to the question in her daughter's eyes. Then Joan's brothers came rushing in, and after them, his face grim, came Jacques d'Arc, her father.

"The Burgundians!" he cried, above the racket of the bells. "Some of the English too. They're riding down the valley to Vaucouleurs."

"The Burgundians!" echoed the boys. Now Catherine was at the door too, her face white.

There was no need for Joan to ask who or why. She knew about the Burgundians. They were men of the next province, born as French as she, but, following their Duke, they had given up all loyalty to the French King, and allied themselves with the English invaders. Off and on, ever since Joan was a baby, they had come riding through the valley, stealing cattle, burning haystacks, spreading terror.

8

But this was something even worse, Jacques d'Arc said now. A courier had just brought the news that the English, far in the west, had ordered a full-scale attack on Vaucouleurs.

Vaucouleurs was the French garrison town down the river which held this small area for the King, and it seemed a long way off to Joan. She had never been there in all her short life. But, listening to her father and her brothers, she realized that twelve miles was not such a distance to galloping soldiers.

"Hurry!" said Jacques d'Arc sharply. "Boys, get the cattle from the fields. Isabelle, you and the girls will gather the provisions together here. Pack what you can. Hide the rest."

"But the captain at Vaucouleurs," said Isabelle faintly. "Will he not fight them off? Hold them back.?"

"Baudricourt?" said Jacques. "He will do his best, no doubt. But when have the French held back the English for long?"

He turned to leave the house again. He was one of the chief men of the village, and it was up to him to help the neighbors prepare for the trouble that was surely coming.

Joan followed him to the door and looked out at the confusion in the road. Men and women were running back and forth, wringing their hands. She saw her father move toward them and raise his voice in authority. Then her mother was calling her to help—put the potatoes in a sack, wrap the bread in cloths.

The hours that followed were strange and exciting. Watchmen were posted in the church tower and at the edge of town. Then the cattle were bellowing in the road, and it was time to start driving them to the old château by the river.

Everyone spent the night there, in the yard of the château, behind the protection of its walls. The next day, some of the men went back to the village to find out if there were any signs of the Burgundians or the English coming nearer. Three days and nights this anxious time of waiting went on.

10

Then, suddenly, there was the sound of galloping hoofs. A single rider, a courier, was posting from Vaucouleurs down the main road to one of the more important towns farther south. Still, he was glad to rein in his horse and give the frightened people of Domremy his news too. They could stop worrying about a raid. The King had signed a treaty with the English King at Troyes. There was going to be peace!

No raid! That was really all anybody heard. The women started crying and laughing. The men slapped each other on the back. And the children danced around in a fine frenzy.

Now as they began the straggling march back to the village the bells set up another clamor, a wild, rejoicing pealing. Soon everyone was gathered in the little church to thank God and all His Saints for saving them from harm.

It was not till later, not till life in Domremy was well back in its usual ways, that the people of the village learned there was no reason at all to rejoice for France and think her troubles were ended.

Joan heard her father talking about it with the other villagers, or with her friendly young uncle, Durand Lassois, when he came to Domremy for a visit.

It was a dreadful peace their King had made. The English claims in France were stronger now than they had ever been. The King—poor, wretched King Charles the Sixth, given for years to fits of madness—had agreed that when he died his crown should go, not to his own son, the young Dauphin, but to the English King. What was more (oh, he must have been mad indeed when he made this treaty), he had even denied that the Dauphin *was* his son.

Joan listened and the words bewildered her. How could the King just give his crown to the enemy? How could he deny his own son?

But she was no more bewildered than everyone else. And, grim as the new peace was, nobody could spend all his time thinking of such matters. Certainly not an eight-year-old girl.

The bells rang and the days passed in their unending round of chores. The seasons passed and there were even times when troubles were forgotten completely. Spring was a time like that, with the air suddenly warm and gentle and a soft green filming all the trees and fields.

The children of Domremy had their own holiday then, a sort of yearly picnic by the Arbre des Dames, a huge old beech tree which stood near a bubbling spring at the edge of town.

Joan went, like all the others. She had a packet of bread and cheese and a winter apple and some nuts in the pocket of her red skirt. Hauviette, her best friend, walked with her, down the road that led past the Old Wood, or Bois Chenu, to the great tree itself.

Joan and Hauviette sat on a little slope to eat their lunch, and they stared off at the tree as they ate. Arbre des Dames—it meant the Fairy Tree.

"Do you believe the fairies dance around it sometimes?" Hauviette asked Joan.

"I never saw them," said Joan flatly, licking cheese off her fingers.

"But your very own godmother did, didn't she?"

"She says so," said Joan. "But I do not hold with fairies and such.

They are all part of sorcery and witchcraft—bad things."

Hauviette nodded, as she generally did when Joan spoke. Then she and Joan both got up to join the other children gathering meadow flowers. When their hands were full, they sat down and braided them into garlands and wreaths. Then they all went to the big beech tree and hung their garlands on its lower branches. Once, long ago, people had done this because they thought the garlands would please the fairies. Now hardly anybody, and surely not Joan, believed in fairies. But it was pleasant to follow the old custom.

After the wreaths were hung, everybody joined hands and began to dance around the tree and sing, Joan's clear voice ringing out more truly than any other.

Oh yes, there were good days along with the troubled ones in Domremy. And Joan enjoyed them along with everyone else. There was nothing remarkable about her at all.

14

Another year passed. And news came to the village that poor, mad King Charles was dead at last. Not only that, the English King to whom he had willed his crown had died at almost the same time. In England, and in Paris and Burgundy, men were proclaiming the dead English King's infant son King of England and France.

"An English baby—King of France," growled Jacques d'Arc. It was too ridiculous for any real Frenchman to consider. The Dauphin was King, no matter what his poor, mad father had said. And now everyone waited for him to prove it, by traveling to the Cathedral in Rheims for his coronation. There he would be anointed with the holy oil of St. Rémy, as every King of France had been since the beginning. Once he had done that no one could deny him any more.

15

Sometimes, when she was out in the fields with the cattle, Joan would think about the journey the Dauphin had to make now. She would sit on a hillside and look off toward the south and west. Far off there, beyond the disloyal province of Burgundy, was the land where the Dauphin was. He would have to leave the safety of that southern country below the Loire River, and travel many miles north to reach Rheims. He would have to ride through land that was held, mile after mile, by the English. But he would do it, Joan thought, God helping him—God and his own patron Saint, the Archangel Michael.

She was so sure of it that she could hardly believe it when news came to the village that the Dauphin had tried—and failed.

She was eleven that summer, and suddenly the battles and troubles nearer home started up again too. Now, for the first time, young men whom Joan herself knew were killed, as Frenchmen again fought French-men near Domremy. All through the fall and the winter and the spring, there were clashes and alarms, and everyone was tired and worn from the constant anxiety. Then in the summer came the news that once again the Dauphin, with an army behind him, had tried to cross the Loire—and failed.

Joan was twelve, old enough to understand very clearly the gloom that settled down on her father and everyone in Domremy. She saw how her father almost despaired now that a day would ever come when a man could till his fields and raise his family in peace.

It was all very unhappy, but what could a little twelve-year-old girl do about it? She could go to church and pray to God and St. Michael and all God's other Saints to have pity on France in her troubles. She could bow her head whenever the bells sounded, and add a prayer for France to her other prayers.

But beyond that—what? Joan did not even wonder, because it was so plain there was nothing.

And then it happened. Then it was that this good, sturdy little girl, who did not even believe in fairies, had the astonishing experience that
16 broke the pattern of her little-girl life forever. She had never been really frightened before, not even when the Burgundians were near. But now she was. For she heard a voice that seemed to come out of thin air, tell-ing her that she was the one who must save France.

"And I was greatly afraid . . ."

I<small>T WAS JUST AN ORDINARY SUMMER DAY, THE DAY IT HAPPENED. JOAN HAD</small> been out in the fields, minding the cattle. Hauviette was with her, and four or five other girls too. Everyone enjoyed being out in the meadows on a sunny, lazy day.

Then the girls saw one of the neighbor boys down by the road, and it seemed to Joan she heard him call, "Your mother wants you."

"All right!" she called back, and made her way home.

But at home, in the cool, dark kitchen, her mother looked at her in surprise. She had sent no message. The boy had been teasing, or perhaps he meant someone else.

So Joan started back toward the meadow. She was crossing the garden back of the house when the bells began their midday ringing. She stopped as always at their sound.

Suddenly, as she listened, she seemed to see a shimmer of light a little to her right, toward the church. Puzzled, she turned her head, and then, out of nowhere, she heard a voice, speaking through the clamor of the bells.

"Attend me, Joan," said the voice. "I come to you from God."

Joan caught her breath and looked about. There was no one in sight. She dropped to her knees, hardly knowing she did so, and her heart was racing. Who was speaking? Who and how?

"I have come from God," the voice repeated, "to help you be good. Go to church, be upright in all your ways, and you can rely on God's protection."

The voice stopped. The shimmer of light vanished. But Joan still knelt there trembling.

It had not been a dream. She was awake, and the voice had been real, sounding in the air as clearly as the bells themselves. But—it had said it came from God. And that was not possible. She was only a little girl—a poor, plain, little country girl.

She began to pray in jumbled, frightened phrases. "Please, dear God, not the Enemy. Save me from bewitchment. Let it not be the Devil, kind Lord, please."

Gradually, it came to her that she had been on her knees in the garden for a long time. What would her mother think if she looked out? She got up and made her way back to the meadow.

All the others were still there, laughing and playing. Joan looked at them as though they were people in a dream.

Hauviette came running up to her. "Is something wrong, Jeanette? You look so pale."

19

Joan looked at Hauviette, trying to make her seem real.

"What is wrong, Jeanette?" asked Hauviette again.

Slowly Joan shook her head. It was impossible to speak of what had happened. "Nothing is wrong," she said. And she went quietly over to the slope and sat down on the grass.

And that was the day that the everyday pattern of Joan's little-girl life ended forever, and a strange new life began.

For the next day she heard the voice again, repeating its first message. Then, the day after that, when she was alone in the fields, there was a vision in the shimmer of light, an awesome, majestic vision of an angel with a flaming sword.

"I am the Archangel Michael," the vision said. "I have come to tell you that God has taken pity on the sufferings of France, and He has chosen you to lead the Dauphin to his crowning. It is you who will ride at the head of the Dauphin's armies to drive the English out of the land."

If Joan had been frightened before, she was overwhelmed now. She cried out in spite of herself, "But I am only a poor girl. What do I know of such things—of soldiering and armies and—and war?"

"God will help you," the vision said. "He will send His Saints to counsel and guide you. St. Catherine and St. Margaret both will come. You may look for them soon."

Then the voice ceased, the vision vanished, and the bells in the village stopped their ringing too.

And then, the next day, the Saints the Archangel had promised did indeed appear. They were gentle, lovely visions, the light around them twinkling like a million tiny stars. And they repeated what the Archangel had said. God had chosen her to save France. But they comforted her too, and told her there was no need to fear. God would help her in her mission, and they themselves would always be near to counsel her.

"Heresy and blasphemy!" the judges were to cry, seven years later, when Joan was on trial for her life. "It is not possible that God would send such visions to an ignorant, untutored girl like yourself. These things were all the invention of your own wicked imagination. Admit it!"

20

The judges lived in a day when people were much less skeptical of mystical experiences than they are now. But even so—Joan's story was too much for them.

Five hundred years and more have passed, and Joan of Arc's story is still a wonder and a mystery. Did she really hear those voices, see those visions?

For some people, it is enough to say yes, it was a true miracle.

But there are others who are uneasy at the idea of miracles. For them, Joan's story has been a worry and a puzzle through the centuries. "She only *thought* she heard those voices," they say. "Only thought she

saw the visions. She was very imaginative—hysterical, perhaps, or ill."
Then they worry some more, because, though mad people *do* have hallucinations, it is simply impossible to write Joan off as mad. "Perhaps," they say then, "like other geniuses, Joan just transformed her own thoughts and desires into voices and visions that seemed to be real and come from outside herself."

So they argue with themselves and with each other, and if they settle the matter to their own satisfaction, they do no harm. And no particular good either.

For not one of their explanations can explain away the most atonishing thing of all—what Joan actually *did* as a result of those voices and visions. In the end, that was the true miracle, which no one can deny.

The first astonishing thing she did was keep what had happened to her a secret for more than four years.

She was only twelve when those voices and visions first appeared, and she was frightened, terribly frightened. But she told no one of her fear. She loved her mother and father, and she had always been a good, obedient daughter, but somehow she never thought of going to them for comfort or reassurance.

She went about her everyday tasks and worried all alone with her immense problem. Had it really been the Archangel, or some dreadful trickery of the Devil?

She would twist the ring she wore on her thumb, the little gold ring her parents had given her that bore the inscription, "Jhesus Maria,"— "All for Jesus and His Mother." The ring had always been a sort of talisman to her, and somehow, holding it, twisting it round and round, was like holding fast to the Faith that had always been the surest thing in her life.

And then, gradually, it began to seem that the voices *must* be telling the truth. They did come from God. Every day she heard them now, and almost every day she saw her Saints. And they were so beautiful, their counsel so good and holy, it was impossible to think they came from the Devil.

So she grew a little quieter, and her eyes were less frightened. And even the terror of the incredible command, that she was the one who had to save France, began to recede a little. Her Saints did not speak of it

often. After once telling her of what her mission would be, they seemed content to ignore it for a while, and speak instead of her daily worries and concerns.

So the days passed, and the seasons passed. People noticed that Joan had grown a little more pious than before, but that was all. Her friend, Hauviette, knew that Joan had vowed she would never be married, but that was not too surprising either. Perhaps she planned to be a nun.

Joan grew to be fourteen, fifteen, and still she gave no sign that anything astonishing had happened to her. She went about her spinning and her sewing, and she was still impatient sometimes, as she had always been. She still lost her temper now and then, and she still cried easily, as she always had.

Then, gradually, her father became aware of something about his daughter that did trouble him.

For a long time he hardly noticed that Joan was always nearby when the talk turned to the troubles of France. He seemed not to see how intently she listened when travelers brought news of the latest English triumphs in the North. Nor how she almost held her breath when people spoke of the Dauphin.

23

It was three years since the Dauphin had made any attempt to cross the Loire and get to Rheims for his crowning. He and his followers drifted from château to château and seemed to have no other plans at all.

"*Nom de Dieu,*" Jacques d'Arc said. "What is he waiting for?"

Joan knew. He was waiting for her. But she gave no sign. Except that as the months went on she showed more and more interest in soldiers. Whenever a soldier rode through town, Joan hurried to gaze at him, studying his horse and his gear. Now and then, trying to sound casual, she would ask questions of her brothers. Exactly how did soldiers lay siege to a town? What were some of the weapons they used?

It was this that finally alarmed Jacques d'Arc.

One day, as Joan was helping her mother in the kitchen, her mother put down her work and looked at Joan. "Your father is very troubled," she said. "He had a strange dream about you last night. He dreamed you—went off with the soldiers."

Joan looked up, too shocked to speak.

Her mother went on quickly, "It was such a foolish dream. I cannot think why he took it so to heart. Only one kind of woman goes off with the soldiers."

"Bad women?" breathed Joan. Suddenly her eyes filled with tears. "Oh, Mother, he thinks that I—that *I*——?"

24

"Shh," said her mother, coming to comfort her. "It was a dream, only a dream. I told him he did wrong even to think of it twice. Our good daughter could never have anything to do with soldiers."

Joan opened her mouth to speak and then closed it again in a sort of anguish. What could she say? She *would* be going off with the soldiers one day, perhaps before too long. Should she tell her mother why? That God had commanded it? Her Saints had never forbidden her to tell her parents. It had been her own choice. But had she been wrong? She stared at her mother desperately.

No, no, she was right not to tell. Her father was worried now, but that worry was nothing to the shock he would feel if he knew the truth. He would try to stop her from doing what she had to do. She knew it. There was nothing for it but to keep her secret, and then, when her mission was truly begun and everyone knew the truth, she would beg her parents to forgive her for her deceit.

But this alarm of her father's did one thing. Joan realized it was time to think seriously of how she could set about carrying out God's command.

She had always been a sensible, practical girl. Now, day after day, she sat at her spinning wheel and she tried to think sensibly and practically about this problem. How could she lead the Dauphin to his crowning?

First she had to get to the Dauphin. He was miles away in Chinon. She would need guides to lead her across the strange and hostile country that lay between. Soldiers would be best. She would need horses too.

Soldiers and horses. Where could she get them? There was only one place—Vaucouleurs. Very well. *Passez Outre*. Go on to the next.

How was she to get to Vaucouleurs? She was sixteen now, but she had never been the twelve miles to that town. She knew her father would never consent to her going there alone.

And then, as she pondered that problem, sickness and sorrow came to the d'Arc house. Joan's older sister, Catherine, became very ill. Before anyone quite realized how ill, she was dead. Joan grieved terribly. For a while everything else was forgotten.

But then, in the sad aftermath, as friends and relatives came from all over to offer their condolences, Joan discovered how she could get to Vaucouleurs. Her uncle, Durand Lassois, fond and kind as far back as

25

she could remember, was one of those visiting relatives. He lived in a town only a mile from Vaucouleurs.

She would ask her uncle to take her home with him for a visit.

And so it was that Joan started out toward Vaucouleurs in the month of May, 1428. She was just sixteen and a half when she began at last to try to merge the two worlds in which she lived and put into practical action the mystical commands of her Saints.

"Since God so commanded,

I had to obey . . ."

JOAN WAS NO LONGER THE LEAST BIT ASTONISHED OR FRIGHTENED BY HER mission. The astonishment, the wonder, and sometimes the fear were all going to be for others from now on.

Durand Lassois was the first.

It was pleasant to have his young niece visiting. His wife had just had a baby, and Joan was a great help around the house. Then, suddenly, one evening after supper, that young niece startled him half out of his wits.

She wanted him to take her to the castle at Vaucouleurs, to see the captain there, Robert de Baudricourt. She had a mission, she said, to save France. She wanted the captain to give her soldiers and horses so she could go to the Dauphin.

Poor Durand was simply staring by this time. So, patiently, Joan went through it all again. "And have you not heard the prophecy, Uncle?" she said. "France having been lost by a woman shall be saved by a maid?"

Stupefied, Durand looked around him and nodded dumbly. It was true, he had heard the saying. And he knew that Isabeau, the German wife of poor King Charles, had added enough to the troubles of France to fulfill the first part of the prophecy easily. But was Joan saying *she* was the maid of the prophecy?

She was. And all the while she was gazing at him with those intense, dark eyes which had always been so hard to resist.

In the end, Durand heard himself agreeing to take her to Captain Baudricourt the very next day.

27

The next day the sun shone, all the flowers of May were blooming
along the road, and the Meuse was silver in the sun. Joan walked along
calmly. She did not look mad, or bewitched, or even nervous. Durand
was nervous enough for both of them.

They came to the town, and walked through it, and up the rise to
the castle. The gates to the castle were open, and the drawbridge was
down. There were sentries here and there but they made no move to
stop Durand and Joan.

They walked right into the castle, Joan leading the way. In a
moment they were in the Great Hall. Durand hung back at the sight of
so many soldiers and other citizens. But Joan paused only a second, looking over the crowd, then she made her way straight to a burly, red-faced
man at the end of the room.

She made a little curtsy, and "You are Robert de Baudricourt,"
she said. It was not a question. She was sure of it.

28

Captain Baudricourt looked at the girl before him and smiled faintly. Here was a neat-looking little thing, he thought, wanting some favor for her father or a sweetheart, no doubt. Then he heard what she was really saying.

It was his turn to be astonished.

She was saying that she had been sent by her Lord with instructions for him and the Dauphin. He was to send the Dauphin word not to let his armies take on the English in battle for a while. The Dauphin was to wait, and then help would come for him from her Lord by mid-Lent of the coming year.

Captain Baudricourt gaped. Orders and instructions for *him*—from this peasant girl in a patched, red skirt?

"And who, may I ask, is your Lord?" he said with heavy irony. "By what right does he give orders to the King?"

"My Lord," answered Joan, "is the King of Heaven."

29

There was a pause. But Captain Baudricourt was only dumfounded for a moment. Then he sighed. Of course, he thought, there were mystics and visionaries everywhere these days. It came from the interminable war. But what was she saying now?

"My Lord has willed that the Dauphin become King in spite of all his enemies can do, and when the time is right it is I who will take him to Rheims to be crowned and anointed."

Now, finally, the captain exploded. He turned to Durand, standing dumb and frightened by Joan's side.

"In the name of Heaven, take her away, man," he cried. "Don't waste my time any more."

He watched as Durand nervously took the girl's arm and hurried her off across the hall. Then, somehow, it was all too much. He burst into laughter and called after them, "Just tell her father to thrash her—and marry her off quickly. That's the best answer for such fancyings."

Outside, Durand and Joan made their way out of the castle yard, back the way they had come. Finally, Durand stole a look at Joan. She did not seem cast down at all. He tried to make some sense of it. And he wondered why she had not asked the captain for soldiers and horses after all, as she had said she would.

Joan's answer hardly helped. She had known, she said, that she would not succeed with Captain Baudricourt at the first approach. In fact, she had a feeling she would have to ask him three times before she got her way. She would come back and ask him again just before Lent next winter, so that help could get to the Dauphin by mid-Lent as she had promised. Meantime, she hoped her good uncle would not feel he must tell her family about all this.

Durand was glad enough to promise that. Actually, he would have been happy to forget the whole business.

But that, of course, was impossible. For now it had begun.

It had begun, even though Joan herself seemed willing to retreat and do nothing more for eight months. Durand might be silent, but there had been other observers of that strange scene in the Great Hall. A certain young lieutenant named Bertrand de Poulengy had been watching, for one. And, absurd as it was, he found himself thinking again and again of the odd, intense girl, with her curious message. There were others, too, who had been impressed.

30

And, of course, there were still others who found the whole thing a good story. In no time, garbled rumors of Joan's visit to the captain had reached Domremy.

It was Jacques d'Arc's turn, and Isabelle's, to feel astonishment and alarm.

They looked at Joan fearfully when she came back from Burey. Alone together they asked themselves what they must do. "*Nom de Dieu*," muttered Jacques, "maybe it is time she was married." He had no idea he was echoing the captain. "Perhaps marriage will put an end to such strangeness."

Together, Jacques and Isabelle decided on a young man whom they thought would make Joan a good husband. Then they broached the subject to Joan, and hit a stone wall. Oh, she was as respectful as always, but long ago, she told them, she had promised God she would live and die a maid.

Jacques d'Arc raged and stormed. She had no right to make such a vow. The old gray house was full of his anger. Then he fell into bitter silence.

And now to all these private miseries in the d'Arc house, there came another misery, this one shared by everyone in Domremy. Suddenly, the lull in the war was over again. Everywhere, the English were on the march.

Had Joan's voices predicted this to her? Was that the reason she had taken the captain's refusal so calmly? Had her voices told her that the troubles of France would grow much worse in the coming months, and had they hinted that, when things were at their darkest, Captain Baudricourt might be less inclined to laugh at a girl offering heavenly help?

Whatever they had said, that was how it happened. In the west, the English were sweeping down on the Loire, hoping to take the Dauphin's last province which lay just beyond it. All the cities along the Loire— Orléans, Blois, La Charité—were girding themselves to resist attack. But more immediate, and more frightening in Domremy, was the news that the English were sending a special force to attack Vaucouleurs.

Hundreds of English and Burgundians at Vaucouleurs? The people of Domremy decided it was hopeless to think the walls of the old château could protect them. In a panic, they packed their most treasured possessions, and, driving their cattle before them, hurried up the river to take refuge in the walled city of Neufchâtel.

32   The d'Arc family joined the pilgrimage, a silent, miserable family, every one of them suffering the results of Joan's stubbornness.

       After a few weeks in Neufchâtel, word came that it was safe to return to Domremy. Captain Baudricourt had signed some sort of truce with the

English. So home they went, to a town of gutted houses, ruined gardens, and a burned and destroyed church.

Oh, they were hard months, those months after Joan's first start on her mission. They were hard for Joan's family, hard for Joan, hard for everyone.

Word came that Orléans was under heavy siege by the English. But the exhausted people of Domremy, struggling to rebuild their own houses, could only sigh for the people of Orléans. And Joan could only wait.

Her voices told her now that it was she who must raise the siege of Orléans. She bowed before this command, accepting it as she accepted everything her Saints said. But it was still not time to go.

And then, at last, in the misty cold of January, just after her seventeenth birthday, they told her it *was* time.

"Go boldly," they whispered, stiffening her back against the knowledge that this time she was leaving for good.

"Good-by," Joan said to her mother and father, giving no hint. Once again she had the excuse of a visit to her Uncle Durand, so, sighing, they watched her go.

"Good-by!" Joan called to Hauviette, as she and Durand passed her house.

Then, soon, she was in Burey again. Durand was ready for her next request. He simply nodded and took her back to Vaucouleurs.

And this time it was a little different than before.

Captain Baudricourt was desperate. The truce he had signed was a limited one. The English would be back soon, and he had received no reinforcements, was no more ready for them than before. He was not laughing at anyone these days, not even village visionaries in patched red skirts. And he remembered Joan.

"All right," he said wearily. "Tell me God's plans for France now."

"You are to give me soldiers and horses," said Joan. "So I can travel to Chinon where the Dauphin is. Meantime, write to him that I am coming to lead his armies to raise the siege of Orléans. After that I will take him to his crowning."

"What?" cried the captain. He had expected some sort of prophesying. That was what he remembered from before.

34

"It is I who will raise the siege of Orléans," Joan repeated.

Oh, it was fantastic! A girl playing at soldiers! "What gives you such mad ideas?" cried the captain angrily.

So now, for the first time to any living soul, Joan told the story of her voices and her visions.

And it did no good.

Captain Baudricourt was quiet for quite a while after she finished. He stared at her, baffled. Then he said, almost sharply, "No, no, it is ridiculous. I am a soldier, after all."

So Joan had her second refusal from Robert de Baudricourt.

But this time she did not leave Vaucouleurs. She went back to the house where she and Durand had taken lodging. She helped the landlady with her spinning. She went every day to church. And she tried very hard to be patient.

It was not easy. It was already February, almost Lent. And the voices of her gentle Saints were almost a clamor now, saying it was time. Joan twisted the ring on her finger, "All for Jesus and His Mother." And she waited for the captain to be convinced.

Still there were others who were paying attention to her. The young soldier, Bertrand, was one. He was more impressed by her this time than before, and he spoke of her to another soldier, Jean de Metz.

One day, as Joan was leaving the church, this Jean saw her and called to her teasingly, "Well, *ma mie*, what are you doing here? Shall the Dauphin be driven from his realm and all of us become English?"

Joan's answer flew at him. She had come for help and was getting none! But it was essential that she get to the Dauphin! And she would get to him, if she had to walk and wear her legs to the knees getting there.

Jean de Metz stared at the girl, his smile quite gone, an odd tingling running up his spine.

What makes for belief? First there is the need, in somebody's heart, for something strong and true to believe in. Then there is something, or someone, who seems to answer that need. Suddenly, to Jean de Metz, and soon to Bertrand too, Joan was that someone, strong, true, and single-hearted, who offered guidance in the midst of chaos.

From mouth to mouth, talk went around Vaucoulers about this dedicated girl, and now there were others who said, "Could it be?"— and, "Why not? Stranger things have happened."

Suddenly one day, Robert de Baudricourt appeared in Joan's lodgings with a priest. He watched intently as the priest approached Joan. If she were a witch, this was the test. She would foam at the mouth and fly away.

Joan did neither. She simply knelt before the priest and asked how he, who had heard her confession, could so doubt her.

Captain Baudricourt stared, muttered—and then went away again.

Now Bertrand and Jean were growing almost as distracted as Joan. There was nothing they would not do for her. Already they had written the letter for her that had been preying on her mind, a letter to her parents, begging their forgiveness for leaving them. What else could they do?

36   "Get me a horse," said Joan abruptly. Now they saw she was going to start without any help from Captain Baudricourt. Eagerly they agreed to go with her and be her escort.

"One more thing," said Joan. "It is not fitting that I should travel

in woman's clothing. I should wear man's dress when I go about a man's work."

From somewhere, Jean de Metz found an outfit for her. Soon Joan was dressed in a boy's doublet and hose. Just being rid of her hampering skirts was like cutting through some of the delays. Quick and neat, she jumped on the horse Bertrand held for her.

And they were away—away!

But they had hardly gone beyond sight of the castle towers when Joan reined in and said it was no good. They must return.

The young men were very patient. They believed in her. They followed her back to Vaucouleurs. And now, once again, Joan went to Captain Baudricourt. This time she told him that on this very day the

37

Dauphin's army had suffered a terrible defeat. "He will have worse," she said, "if you do not give me my proper escort and send me to him soon."

Then she went back to her lodgings and waited again. In just a few days, couriers came to the captain with the news that the Dauphin's forces had indeed known a terrible defeat on February 12, the day Joan had told him so.

What makes for belief? There is a need, and an answer to the need, and then, for some people, a sign is needed too. The captain had had his sign. Shaken and confused, he began to get an escort ready for Joan; Jean, Bertrand, and four other soldiers.

The townspeople were all convinced by Joan now. Eagerly they brought her a brand-new doublet and hose to wear. And Joan herself had her hair cut like a soldier's, round as though a pudding bowl had been clapped on her head. She did not look beautiful. She did not want to. What need had a soldier for that?

Still, there was something in those dark eyes of hers, as she sat on her horse before the castle of Vaucouleurs, that *was* beautiful. Jean and Bertrand, on their horses, looked at her, and did not see her as a girl in boy's clothes. They did not see her as a girl at all, but the strange, unlikely embodiment of hope itself.

Captain Baudricourt came forward with a sword he had had especially made for Joan. He hung it on her belt. Then he looked up at her and sighed, and said, "Go, and let come what will."

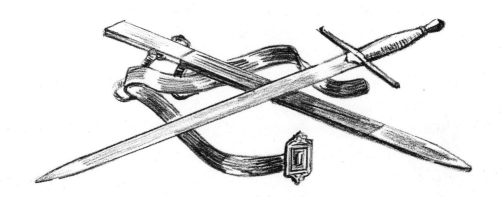

"And I knew him at once,

among many . . ."

AT LAST SHE WAS ON HER WAY TO MEET HIM, THE ONE ON WHOM HER thoughts had been fixed for almost five years now, the Dauphin. She was wrapped in such relief she hardly thought about the hazards of the journey.

Bertrand and Jean fretted anxiously around her. They must travel by night rather than by day. They must wrap the horses' hoofs in cloth to muffle their sound. They must always keep one lookout even when they slept.

Joan smiled and nodded to everything they said. Nor did she complain at the cold, or the rain, and the endless mud. Only one thing troubled her. She wished they could stop more often to hear Mass. There were chapels and churches all along the way. But Bertrand and Jean would not hear of it. Did she not know, they asked her, how far her fame had spread already? Yes, even here in Burgundy they had heard of her.

"But I have done nothing yet," said Joan.

"People know about you," they answered. "Did not Dunois, the Defender of Orléans, write twice about you to de Baudricourt? If your name is known in Orléans, it is known here."

So Joan sighed and submitted to their judgment. Night after cold, dark night, mile after cold, wet mile, they traveled, and at last they came to Gien, on the Loire. They were in the Dauphin's own country here, the land that was truly France. And it was like a small miracle to their escort that they had come all across hostile Burgundy without one real alarm.

Now they could travel by day and more swiftly. Joan could even stop to hear Mass at the Chapel of St. Catherine in Fierbois. Finally, eleven days after they had left Vaucouleurs, they came to the towers and battlements of Chinon.

It was a city of magic to Joan. She caught her breath, not just at the splendor of its castle, but because somewhere in those clustered towers, behind those massive walls, lived the man God willed to be King of France.

Bertrand and Jean took her to the village below the castle, and found lodgings for her, and then went forth to see about arranging a meeting for her with the Dauphin.

In her room, Joan fasted and prayed, and listened as Bertrand and Jean brought in their reports. Was it going to be the story of Vaucouleurs all over again? One delay after another?

Certainly it started out that way. The Dauphin had two advisors, Regnault, the Archbishop of Rheims (he was far from his Cathedral; in fact, had never been near it), and another called La Trémoïlle. These two needed endless conferences, it seemed, before admitting Joan to the castle. Joan pressed her lips together, and twisted her ring, and held onto her patience.

Then, suddenly, curiosity triumphed at the castle. Word came that Joan was expected at once.

She mounted her horse and rode swiftly up the hill. In the castle yard she dismounted, and walked steadily to the great doors where a velvet-clad courtier was waiting to lead her to the Dauphin.

In a sudden flutter of panic she looked up at him and said, "You will not try to mislead me, sir?" The courtier stared at her with an odd look on his face, and then hurried her on.

They came to the Great Hall. It was ablaze with torches and crowded with the great and small of the Dauphin's court. Silks, satins, and velvets gleamed in a kaleidoscope of colors, jewels flashed and filmy veils floated like mist from the pointed hats of the ladies.

But the dazzle was only a blur to Joan, standing there in her gray doublet and hose. She was looking for one person only.

Across the Hall, a richly dressed man sat on a carved throne. A path was open through the crowd. Joan looked, frowned, then glanced along the row of figures on either side of the throne.

Suddenly she moved forward and made her way to a man half-hidden in the shadows. She stopped before him, made a curtsy that went oddly with her boy's clothes, and said, "Gentle Dauphin, I am Joan the Maid."

The man before whom she had stopped was a poor, ramshackle figure, with anxious, watery eyes, and loose, full lips. He stared at her stupidly, and then said, "It is not I who am King, Joan. There is the King." He pointed to the throne. There was a hush.

Joan never wavered. *"Nom de Dieu,"* she said beseechingly. "It is you, noble Prince, and none other."

The young man drew a deep breath and then looked around the court with a proud, wondering smile. A murmur ran through the Hall like a rising wind. "She did it." "She knew him."

They *had* tried to mislead her, for a test, or a game, but it did not matter. She knew him anyway, in spite of the fact that he looked so little like anyone's dream of a king.

"My voices told me," she said later. And indeed, to everyone in the Hall, it seemed plain already that some sort of miracle had taken place. Regnault, the hawk-nosed Archbishop, and the fat La Trémoïlle, stared, incredulous and angry, as the young man who had been their own particular property put his hand on Joan's arm and led her aside to a curtained alcove.

Joan's face was radiant as she followed him. What grandeur did she see in him that nobody else in France could see?

In the privacy of the alcove, she sought to give him the faith in her that he must have.

"God has sent me to lead your armies to the relief of Orléans," she

said. "And then, gentle Dauphin, I will take you to your crowning."

The Dauphin blinked his watery eyes. He knew this was why she had come. It was the talk of the court. He was impressed that she had recognized him. But still, that was hardly a great enough sign for a doubting fellow like himself.

So now Joan told him of her visions and voices. Then, when he still frowned and blinked, she said, "Very well. I will give you a sign that I truly come from God." Then she told him of a prayer he had prayed, alone in his chapel, a whole year past, when his life had seemed at its darkest moment.

At last his face lightened and seemed to grow firmer. How could this girl have known of that prayer, except from God and His Saints?

He led her out into the Great Hall again, and everyone could see by his face that this strange girl had won him. They crowded about her and murmured happily when the Dauphin called servants to prepare a fine room. Joan was to stay at the castle.

It should have been easy after that. It seemed to Joan that it should

43

only be a matter of days before the Dauphin's troops were readied, and she would be riding off to Orléans.

Alas for Joan, to whom it always seemed that the logical next step would be as clear to others as it was to her. To the Dauphin, it seemed he had already gone very far. The logical next step was to get everybody's agreement that he had not done wrong.

So the days passed and became weeks, and once again Joan's patience was tested almost to the breaking point.

Oh, it was not all bad. She was only seventeen after all. And the Dauphin, in his own confused way, was eager to be friendly. The day after she came, he led her out into the courtyard to show her a beautiful horse that would be hers from now on. Joan leaped onto the horse and galloped to the end of the yard and back, and it was as though she had been born knowing how to ride a horse like this. Everyone marveled at her skill.

She made friends too. The same day she was given her horse, the young Duke d'Alençon arrived at the castle. Somehow, at one glance, Joan and the handsome young man knew they were friends. The Duke told the Dauphin that he would gladly ride into battle at Joan's side. *"Mon beau Duc,"* Joan called him fondly, and, when she met his pretty wife, she loved her too, and told her she need not worry about her husband's safety in battle, when she, Joan, was near.

She was a little like a mother to her *"beau duc,"* and a little like a younger sister, listening wide-eyed as he told her of battles and tourneys and taught her fine points of horsemanship.

But here at the castle there was always news from the embattled towns of France. Here Joan was right beside the Dauphin when couriers came from Orléans. The people of that city were close to starving now, the couriers said. Dunois, Orléans' defender, prayed that the Dauphin would at least send food if he could not send troops to raise the siege.

"Let me go," Joan cried, "let me go."

"Well, but not just yet," said the Dauphin. She had made certain claims, after all, that she came from God. Therefore, it was necessary that she go to Poitiers and be examined by a panel of churchmen there. Only with their approval could the Dauphin be absolutely sure that this maid was not, in all good faith, herself deceived about her mission.

So off they went to Poitiers, the Dauphin and a whole train of

44

courtiers accompanying Joan. Joan was quiet as the monks and priests
who had gathered under the leadership of Regnault began to question
her. But gradually her answers grew quicker.

"Give us a sign you come from God," they insisted.

"Nom de Dieu!" she answered, in an echo of her father's old impatient cry. "Let me go to Orléans and you shall have your sign!"

And again they asked, "If it is God's intention to deliver France, as
you say, what *need* can there be of armed troops?"

45

"Nom de Dieu," cried Joan, growing distracted. "The armed men will do the fighting and God will give the victory!"

Still the churchmen kept on. But at last, impressed in spite of themselves by her sincerity and honesty, they wrote up their conclusions, which "no man should deny without disregarding the will of God." The Maid had been examined as to her life, her conduct, her intentions, and found in all things, humble, pious, and simple. Regnault himself signed the findings.

"Now!" said Joan. "Now!"

But now it seemed there was still one more necessary examination, and for this she must go to Tours.

Would she go out of her wits with impatience? No. Her voices still came to her, morning, noon, and night. They were with her when the clerics questioned her. They were with her always.

So she stayed desperately calm. She asked only that one of the clerks write a letter for her, "since she herself knew not A from B." "A letter to whom?" the churchmen asked.

"To the English," she replied. Again there was a great frowning and consulting. But finally they agreed.

Joan told the clerk exactly how to address the letter: "To the Duke of Bedford in Paris, and to his lieutenants before the gates of Orléans." Then she went on, dictating as firmly as though she had been writing letters to regents and generals all her life long. "To all of you! Deliver up the keys of all the good towns you have taken in France. Go away, back to your own country; otherwise, await news of the Maid, who will soon visit you to your great detriment."

Then she was willing to go to Tours.

And there, at last, the Dauphin began to assemble armor for her and equipment. It was really impossible to hesitate any longer. She had passed every test, spiritual and physical. More than that, there were hundreds, there were thousands who believed in her now, where once there had been only Bertrand and Jean.

For years the need of all these people had been growing, till it was like an aching hunger for someone to make things simple again, and good and true. In Poitiers, in Tours, everywhere she went, Joan seemed the answer to that need.

She was no longer a little country girl, Jeannette of Domremy, with a strange idea of her mission. She was the hope of France, Joan the Maid. The Dauphin could ignore it no more.

She asked for white armor, armor, that is, without any of the elaborate engraving on it that some knights liked. And she asked for a standard, a fluttering sign to which her men could rally in battle. Carefully, she told the standard maker just how to fashion it, of white with a silken fringe. On one side, on a field of lilies, was to be pictured the King of Heaven, and over His head, the motto from Joan's ring, "Jhesus Maria." The other side was to be a field of azure and on it a silver dove. Later, Joan asked for a banner too, for her priest.

For she had a priest of her own now, who seemed to have come, like a miracle, straight from her mother. He was Brother Pasquerel, a monk of Tours, who had met her mother on a pilgrimage from which he had just returned. He came to Joan with her mother's love and forgiveness, and her father's too. And he promised to stay by Joan's side as long as she needed him. With him had come two of her brothers, Jean and Pierre, anxious to fight for France under their sister's banner.

47

Joan had a squire too, Jean d'Aulon, a wiry young man, full of energy and devotion. A priest, a squire, a page—she had everything she needed but a sword. And suddenly she gave a strange order about that. "Send," she said to the Dauphin, "to the Chapel of St. Catherine, in Fierbois. Have the monks dig in the earth behind the altar. They will find there the sword I want."

The Dauphin sent word to the chapel, and the monks dug, and lo, there was the sword just as Joan had predicted. It was another miracle for the people who were ready to expect anything from her now.

Now she was ready—to ride out with her "*beau duc*" and the generals and the army. They had a great train of provisions for Orléans, six hundred wagons of foodstuffs and four hundred head of cattle.

It was the last part of April, 1429, almost the end of Lent, and Joan was on her way to raise the siege of Orléans.

"I told my men

to have no fear . . ."

SHE RODE ON HER WHITE HORSE, AT THE HEAD OF THREE THOUSAND men, and her raging confidence was like a wind that swept them all after her. At night, when they broke their march, the soldiers knelt at her command, to confess and hear Mass. In the morning they rose to hear Mass again, and not one of them murmured at the strangeness of it.

Then, on the second day of their march, in the stormy afternoon of Thursday, April 28, they came within sight of the spires and walls of Orléans. And suddenly Joan was in a panic, because it seemed she had been tricked by the generals.

It was her first hint of the difficulties she was to have with the generals all during the next week. Perfectly willing to have her along as a sort of mascot, these officers were fiercely jealous of any commands she might give. And they had followed their own ideas in the approach of Orléans.

Joan did know this much about the besieged city. It lay on the northern bank of the Loire, and was surrounded by a wall in which there were four gates. There was also a bridge leading across the Loire to the southern bank. So, there were five entrances to the city—in theory. Actually, there was only one by which the relieving troops could hope to bring in supplies for the city—the Burgundy Gate in the eastern wall. The English had ringed the city round with forts, but they had skimped on the eastern side. Only one fort guarded the road to the Burgundy Gate.

49

Since Joan and the army were approaching from the east, Joan had asked the generals to follow the northern bank of the river straight toward that gate.

Instead, she discovered now that they had marched toward Orléans on the southern bank, and there they were, within sight of the city, but with the river lying between.

The rain poured down and a mean wind blew from the west, riffling the water against the current. Joan's new armor hurt her, and, as always when alarmed, she was in a temper.

Dunois, the Defender of Orléans, had hastily crossed the river to greet her. He came hurrying up.

50   "I rejoice to see you, Joan," he cried.

Joan frowned, her eyes flashing. "Was it by *your* order I was brought to this side of the river? Is this how you make use of the best help ever offered a city—the help of God Himself?"

Anxiously Dunois tried to explain. He was a handsome, brave, and patient young man, related to Joan's favorite, the Duke d'Alençon. And though he himself had not planned this march, he had figured out a perfectly sensible next step. A fleet of sailing barges was to sail up the river to the spot where the cattle and provisions had been halted. The barges would transport these supplies down the river to protected moorings by the Burgundy Gate.

But alas! it was not Dunois' fault that the wind had been blowing steadily from the west since yesterday. The sailing barges could not tack upstream against the current, so long as the wind blew with them.

The Duke d'Alençon came up. A whole group of long-faced generals appeared. They were fearful now that the English across the river would soon catch sight of the halted supplies and send a force to capture them.

Suddenly, Joan's mood changed. She was reassuring the worried officers. "Be not so troubled. The wind will change, gentlemen," she said, and turned away, no longer concerned.

The generals looked at each other, annoyed more than anything.

Then Dunois lifted his head. He raised one hand to feel the wind, and an incredulous look came over his face. A cry came from all the officers as they stared toward the river. For a moment, it seemed as though the water, blown upstream, had halted in a peaked wall. Then it was rushing downstream in a pouring flood.

The wind had changed. It was sweeping in from the east.

Was it a miracle, or wasn't it? The generals murmured and frowned, but it was not really enough to change their minds. Winds do change, sooner or later.

Actually, to Dunois, it seemed more of a miracle later on, when he was guiding the barges upstream, close by the English in the Fort de St. Loup, and the English made no move to fire on the little fleet.

It was too late to load the barges that night. They were loaded next day and sent downstream.

And that evening Joan herself entered Orléans by the Burgundy Gate. She was still a little angry. The mixup about the approach had meant that the army had had to retire up the river eastward again, to cross over and come down the northern bank, just as she had wanted in the beginning. She had parted from her soldiers anxiously, sending Brother Pasquerel with them to keep them in a state of grace.

But as she entered Orléans she grew happier in spite of herself. Everyone had turned out to greet her and honor her. For six long months these people had been pent up in their city. Now Joan, God's own messenger, had come to rescue them.

Joan went to bed that night in the home of one of Orléans' chief citizens, and she already knew what she was going to do first.

Next morning, Dunois hurried off up the river to oversee the return of the troops with plenty of reinforcements. And Joan called a scribe and began to dictate a letter. She was going to give the English every chance to surrender peacefully before any attack was made.

52   Her letter was very like the first she had written them. "Give up. Go back where you came from, for that is God's will!"

The English sent back no reply. They knew that only a handful of soldiers remained with Joan in the city. It was a wonderful opportunity for them to storm the city and capture the maid who was already notorious. Why didn't they? Instead, they simply kept the heralds who had delivered Joan's letter and shouted a few insults toward the city.

That evening Joan tried again. She went a short way out onto the bridge that spanned the Loire. At the far end of the bridge the English had built one of their strongest forts, Tourelles. Joan called across the broken span that separated the northern end of the bridge from Tourelles. "Give up!" she called. "Go away and your lives will be spared."

"Hussy!" the English captain bellowed back. All the English soldiers took up the cry. "Hussy! Cowgirl!" She worried them, but still they could not take her seriously.

Joan burst into tears at the things they yelled, and went back to her lodgings, still crying.

But the next day she tried again. Then at last word came that the French army, greatly increased, was returning. At dawn, on the fourth morning after her arrival, Joan rode out to welcome Dunois and all the eager troops hurrying to her standard.

The English in the Fort de St. Loup watched the troops pour into the city and did not fire a shot. But in Orléans the air was crackling with excitement. Soon now, things would begin to happen.

It was about ten o'clock that same morning. The troops were being settled in their billets. And, after warning Dunois that she would be cross indeed if the generals took any action without letting her know, Joan had gone to her room to rest. Her squire, d'Aulon was already asleep on a cot.

But in just a few minutes, Joan was on her feet in a frenzy.

"Nom de Dieu!" she was crying. "My voices tell me I must go—go against the English! But they do not say where! At one of their forts? Or are some reinforcements on their way?"

D'Aulon sat up on his cot, staring in bewilderment.

"Move!" Joan cried to him. "Oh, where are those whose business it is to arm me? Where? And all the while, the blood of our people is reddening the ground!"

D'Aulon got up and began rushing around, helping Joan into her armor. Brother Pasquerel hurried in, but now Joan was rushing out. D'Aulon followed her, and then, in the street before the house Joan stopped and cried, "My standard! My standard!"

53

From the window above, someone leaned out and thrust her standard through the opening. Joan grasped it, leaped onto her horse, and was away in such a rush that her horse's hoofs struck sparks from the cobbles.

After all the delays and confusions of the past days, Joan was riding out into action at last!

Straight for the Burgundy Gate she rode, led by some instinct, and there she saw a wounded Frenchman lying on the cobbles.

D'Aulon caught up with her now, and saw her terrible face. "Never," she cried, "do I see a wounded Frenchman but my hair stands straight up on my head! Come!" And she galloped out of the gate toward the Fort de St. Loup.

It was clear very soon what had happened. It was no trick of the generals, after all. Some of the newly arrived troops had been too eager to stay in their billets. They had rushed out, with no plan, to attack the

54

fort. Rousing themselves at last from their enchantment, the English had begun to defend themselves. Now the French were falling back.

Then they caught sight of Joan galloping toward them, her white standard streaming above her.

"The Maid!" they cried. *"L'Angélique!"* And as the cry swept through the troops, the men who had begun to retreat turned to go forward again, following Joan. From the gate of the city came a stream of soldiers too, hurrying to Joan's standard.

Suddenly, in the space of minutes, the mood of the fighting around Orléans changed. Before this, whatever happened, the English had seemed the victors. Now, as the French surged after Joan's white banner toward the fort, they were the conquerors!

An hour, two hours, they fought. Joan riding back and forth among them, urging them on. "Go boldly," she cried. "Have no fear! Forward —forward—they are ours!"

Recklessly, the French raised their ladders against the walls, and swarmed up them, heedless of English hatchets and stones. A burst of flame flared in the fort. The French had it! It was theirs!

By Vespers, it was all over. The Fort de St. Loup was in ruins, and Joan was praying for the souls of the hundred and fourteen Englishmen who had been killed.

Everyone in the city was full of joy and hope. The soldiers were talking of how they would do even worse to the English on the morrow. The generals were already planning which of the remaining ten forts they would attack next.

And then Joan sent out a herald to proclaim that, since the next day was a Holy Day, there would be no fighting at all.

Perhaps the generals did have some reason to be exasperated with her. They did not understand Joan's kind of war, with God's commands taking precedence over all others. Murmuring and fretful, they granted her her Holy Day. But they watched with scorn as she sent still another letter to the English. This one she wrapped around an arrow, and had it shot by a crossbow man into the English camp. But she still got only shouts in reply.

The day after that, the generals took over again. And at once got involved in a retreat!

Their plan had been to head across the river, over a bridge of little boats, to attack the easternmost fort on the southern bank, one of two which guarded Tourelles.

Joan was delayed in getting her horse across the river. By the time she arrived on the southern bank the French forces already there were starting back again.

"*Nom de Dieu,*" she cried. "What has happened?"

Frowning, she listened to the hurried explanations. The English had evacuated the first fort and retired to make a strong stand in the next one to the west. The prudent generals seeing the English forces doubled by this move, had decided it was foolish to attack without reinforcements.

Joan and a reckless young captain who was with her simply stared at each other for a moment. Then they both couched their lances and spurred their horses forward, toward the English in their farther fort.

Only for a moment did they gallop alone. D'Aulon suddenly spurred his horse and followed them. Then another turned to follow and another. It was as though no Frenchman *could* retreat when Joan's white banner led the way.

In no time, all the French forces were surging toward the English in the Fort des Augustins, and the English were hurrying to defend it as well as they could.

All day the battle raged, and that evening Joan and the army watched as the English gave up the Fort des Augustins and retreated hurriedly behind the earthworks that guarded the great fort on the bridge.

Again the bells rang in Orléans and everyone rejoiced. Two English forts had been abandoned in one day!

Weary but happy, Joan was eating supper when a messenger came from the generals. Actually, it was beginning to seem that nothing made them more uneasy than the possibility of success. They had taken counsel, the messenger said, and decided that nothing more could be done now, without reinforcements.

Joan was silent a moment, her lips tight. Then she spoke to the messenger.

"Tell the generals that they have had their counsel, and I have had mine. Be assured that mine, which comes from the Lord, will be fulfilled."

She turned to Brother Pasquerel, who sat at her side. "Please rise even earlier tomorrow," she said. "And stay close beside me all day. I shall have much to do. And besides"—her voice faltered a moment, then went on steadily—"I shall be wounded tomorrow—before the fort on the bridge."

There was a hush in the room. Silently, uneasily, the messenger departed. Silently, pensively, everyone went to bed.

The generals had taken their counsel, Joan had taken hers. Then next morning it turned out that the citizens had taken theirs. At dawn a delegation of them came to Joan. Their counsel matched with hers. They wanted her to take command and continue the attacks on the English.

"Most willingly!" cried Joan. She was already in her armor and she started for the door.

"Joan!" cried her hostess beseechingly. All night she had thought about the wound Joan had predicted. "Must you go out—so swiftly? Stay, stay and eat first!"

"You may save my breakfast," said Joan. "I will bring back an Englishman to share it this evening, and we will come back to Orléans—across the bridge!"

So she rode out, and now, all of a sudden it was plain the generals had changed their minds *again*. As she cantered toward the gate, they came riding after her, and then all the forces in the city fell in behind.

Once again they crossed the river on the bridge of little boats, for Tourelles was the goal today!

With Joan spurring them on, the soldiers ran toward the earthworks

that protected Tourelles as though there were no such thing as death. Huddled under their strange, tortoise-like shields, they ran toward the moat the English had dug before the earthworks and hastened to fill it with bundled brush.

Stones, lances, hatchets, and maces fell about them as they struggled in and out of the moat. The English were fighting desperately to defend Tourelles. Hour after hour, the French persisted, pushing forward, falling back.

Then Joan herself was down in the moat. She had grabbed a ladder. At the far side of the moat she flung the ladder against the English ramparts.

She had a foot on the first rung when a bolt from a crossbow came whistling down from the English ranks above. It struck her just under the right shoulder, and she fell to the ground.

At once Dunois was at her side, then her squire, and Brother Pasquerel. Quickly, they hurried her back across the moat and away from the fiercest fighting. Then they sat her down and began to loosen her armor.

Joan's face was pale and frightened. She had expected the wound

but she had not expected it to hurt so much. Tears ran down her cheeks, and as she moaned softly those around her felt like weeping too.

But her weakness lasted only a moment. Then she set her teeth and reached up to pull forth the bolt with her own hands. She winced at the gush of blood, but she was quiet and steady as they applied a dressing.

Then Dunois looked toward the moat and the hard-pressed soldiers and sighed. "We have done all we can for one day. I will sound retreat."

"*Nom de Dieu!*" cried Joan, on her feet with the wound forgotten. "You would sound retreat with the battle almost won?"

"Joan, look," protested Dunois. "Everywhere we are falling back."

"Give me fifteen minutes by myself," said Joan. "Let the soldiers rest a while and eat and drink. Then—then—there will be a sign! Follow me then!"

It was senseless. But with Joan's eyes burning on him Dunois suddenly gave in. He went to tell the soldiers to rest. And Joan went aside to an old vineyard nearby and knelt to pray.

Then—who knew exactly how it happened?—d'Aulon was holding Joan's standard for her. He and another soldier were standing idly, and all at once the two of them started toward the moat. They scrambled down into the brush that filled it. As they slipped and stumbled, Joan's standard wavered, leaned forward—touched the wall of the rampart.

From her distance, Joan looked up and saw it. "My standard!" she cried, and leaped up and ran toward it.

"My standard!" The sweet, piercing cry echoed over the field. The soldiers looked up, saw the banner, saw the Maid herself leaping into the ditch, then suddenly reappearing on the far side, brandishing her flag.

Then it was as though they were all propelled by magic. They rose and swept toward the moat. All afternoon it had stopped them. Now they simply swarmed into, across it, and then flung up their ladders and climbed them as though they were climbing stairs.

The English above them stood staring dumfounded. They had seen the Maid fall, wounded. They had seen the soldiers retreating. Now here they were, popping up all along the wall.

60   At last the English came to life and began to fight back. But it was too late.

"Surrender!" cried Joan. "Yield yourself!" she cried to the captain who had shouted so many insults at her.

"Never!" the captain shouted back. Now he started his men retreating into the fort on the bridge, Tourelles itself. A short wooden span led from the rampart on the riverbank to this fort.

And now an unknown French hero added a master stroke. As the English soldiers milled across the span, a fireboat suddenly floated under the little bridge.

The fire flared up. Wild flames from tar, resin, and cotton waste engulfed the short span. There were shrieks and cries, then the thunder of cracking timber—and the bridge collapsed. All the English who were on it tumbled into the Loire.

61

Joan's face was white in the light of the fire. Even as the heavily armored English vanished under the turmoil of the water, she was crying and murmuring, "God save their poor souls."

Meantime, while the English were meeting destruction at the southern approach to Tourelles, the citizens of Orléans began rushing onto the bridge at its northern end, running toward the northern walls of the fort. A span was gone in the middle of the bridge. Never mind! Eager hands relayed lengths of timber. Were they long enough? Just barely. One brave man was running across the makeshift span—then another, and another! From both ends of the bridge now, the French were converging on Tourelles.

The English stood in a daze. Now it seemed *they* saw visions. Not only did they see the Maid, with her luminous white banner, but it seemed that at the head of the soldiers and citizens streaming toward them, there were shining Saints, riding horses white as lilies!

As one man, all the English who were still alive threw down their arms.

It was over.

That night, the night of May 7, Joan did go back into Orléans across the bridge, just as she had promised.

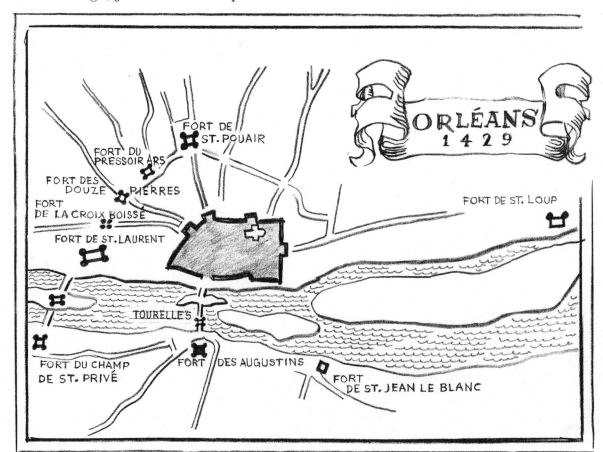

"My standard shared the dangers

. . . why not the honors too?"

THE NEXT DAY JOAN, THE ARMY, AND ALL THE TOWNSPEOPLE WATCHED as the remaining English in the six forts on the western side of Orléans, marched out onto the plain, lined up, wheeled, and marched away.

The siege of Orléans was over.

Nine days after the arrival of a seventeen-year-old girl with no experience in warfare, the impossible had been done. Orléans was free.

Never had there been such a holiday as that Sunday was in Orléans, and never such a heroine as Joan. The tumult of delight and rejoicing was so great that it echoes down to this day when May the 8th is still celebrated as the Feast of Joan the Maid.

As for Joan herself, the tide of love swirled about her, and she smiled and was pleased. But there was not the slightest danger of her head being turned by the praise of earthly voices when the same sweet voices she had heard in the quiet of Domremy still whispered in her ears.

Accompanied by her unseen Saints, she rode or walked about the city, and she frowned when men and women begged to touch her ring that they might be blessed. "You will be blessed as much by touching your own rings," she said crossly. "*I* have worked no miracles. It is God."

She was still Joan, brisk and practical, unable to see anything the

63

least bit astonishing about herself. And already she was impatient to be on with the rest of her mission. Within a day after the English had left Orléans, Joan was riding away too, hurrying back to the Dauphin. It was time, at last, to lead him to his crowning.

So she rode toward Tours, where the Dauphin and his court were staying. As she came close to the city, the Dauphin himself rode out to greet her.

As always, she was dazzled by him, and bowed her head low over her horse's mane as he approached. But the Dauphin called out to her to sit erect. He drew his horse alongside hers and held out both hands to her, and Joan's face shone with happiness.

Oh yes, he was pleased with what she had done, and told her so gladly. But as for hurrying on at once toward Rheims—well, now, that was something else again. He blinked and looked about anxiously for his long-time advisors.

So now it all began again, the same old pleading and waiting that Joan had known before Orléans.

The Dauphin loved to travel from one fine château to another, fleeing the necessity to settle down with one thought in one place. He was off again now, and Joan followed him patiently.

"Please, gentle Dauphin," she besought him, "let us give up this aimless traveling and go north, to your crowning."

"But, Joan," protested the Dauphin, "you know we are discussing the matter. We are discussing it every day."

Indeed it was so. There were discussions that seemed as though they might go on forever. Looking back on them now, across the years, it seems idiotic that there could have been so many different opinions about what the Dauphin should do next. Charles the Sixth had been dead for nine years. His son had still not been crowned. No wonder men doubted that he was the rightful King.

Finally one day, Joan rapped on the door of the Dauphin's private counsel room. When the Dauphin called, "Come in!" Joan ran in and knelt at his feet.

64   "Gentle Dauphin," she cried, "do you want to know what my voices say about this matter? They say," her voice rose, "they say, 'Daughter of God, go—go—go! We will give you our aid, only *go!*'"

Blinking and falling back a little, the Dauphin seemed overwhelmed

at last. Very well, he said, he would go. That is, he would go if—first Joan
and the army would recover a couple of cities on the Loire from the
English.

Only the capture of two or three cities between her and her goal?
Joan was like a whirlwind!

Her "*beau duc*" was the chief commander of the army that marched
out toward the Loire, and Joan rode beside him, her white standard flying.
They were going first to Orléans, which would be their base.

The people of Orléans were in a frenzy of delight to see her again and they had fine gifts for her. Joan smiled with pleasure at the crimson cloak, the green velvet tunic, the gold sword belt. She might dress like a soldier, but she was a girl after all, who loved the look and touch of silk and velvet.

Then, her crimson cloak about her, she and the Duke d'Alençon and the army rode out to take a town called Jargeau. Once again, as so often, there was a cautious council of captains who had heard the English were expecting reinforcements. Once again, as so often, the French floundered at first, confused by a bold English sally.

But then, as at Orléans, Joan rode out, and at the sight of that small, brave figure, the sound of that sweet, floating voice, the French troops were inspired.

"Were you afraid, my duke?" Joan called to the Duke d'Alençon as they came near together in the melee. "Have you forgotten my promise to your wife, that I would send you home safe and sound?"

The Duke smiled at her, shamefaced. But later that same day he saw her riding toward him again. "Move from that spot!" she called sharply. "Move! Move quickly, or you will be killed by that gun on the rampart above you!"

Almost without thinking, the Duke did move. A little later he saw with awe and horror another man struck dead, standing in that same place. After that, the Duke was like a man possessed, fighting as if to take the town for Joan singlehanded.

That same day Joan herself was struck from a scaling ladder by a falling stone. But she was on her feet again in an instant. And an hour later the town was won, the English general surrendering himself to the girl he called "the bravest woman in the world."

A day's rest in Orléans, and then Joan and the army were riding out to take another town. June 15, June 16, June 17, on every day there was a victory, the last one a triumph known to history as Patay. On that field over two thousand Englishmen were killed or taken prisoner, and among the prisoners was Lord Talbot who had been chief commander at Orléans.

66

Weary and triumphant, Joan rode back to the château where the Dauphin was waiting, and told him she was ready now to lead him to Rheims.

The Dauphin looked at her and bit his lips. "Joan, Joan," he said, "how you have worked for me! What you must do now is—rest!"

Rest! Joan stared at him, astounded. Then her hands flew to her face and she burst into terrible sobs. She could not help herself. What was she to do with this man? God willed him to be King of France and commanded her to make him so. But how? She had tried patience, and pleading, and winning him what he wanted. Nothing did any good.

Later, her *"beau duc"* tried vainly to comfort her. She should remember the Dauphin had no money to pay the troops. She should remember Rheims itself was hardly loyal.

It was no good. Joan was beside herself. Suddenly, with just a few companions, she rode away from the château. Her lips tight, she led her little group off into the fields. There she had the men pitch camp for her. Out there in the middle of nowhere, she sat herself down and spoke to no one.

Perhaps the Dauphin was just waiting for something like that. At any rate, two days later he started. At last, with his court and his army, he began the march to Rheims.

Her mood changing in a moment, Joan joyfully told her companions to break up the camp, and they rode to join him.

There were indeed hazards ahead. Hostile Burgundy had to be crossed, Burgundy studded with cities which barred their gates to the Dauphin and his army, refusing them needed provisions.

Bold as always, Joan would have challenged them all. But La Trémoïlle liked long parleys which ended with him receiving pleasant sums of gold in exchange for a guarantee of no fighting.

La Trémoïlle had his way once, but then Joan held firm, and one city after another, faced by an ultimatum from the Maid, decided to open its gates and give the Dauphin what was needed.

At last they came close to Rheims. They halted some miles away till word came that the city was opening its gates for the Dauphin, the Maid and the army.

On Saturday, July 16, the way was clear. The gates of Rheims were opened, and the streets of the city were crowded with excited people. And at the sight of the Maid, riding beside the Dauphin, enthusiasm and rejoicing grew in a mounting wave.

The coronation was scheduled for the very next day. All the rest of

67

that day, all that night, the citizens of Rheims worked in a fever, ready-
ing the city and the Cathedral. And all through the humming hours Joan
moved in a dream.

Familiar faces moved through the dream, not just those recently
known, but dearer ones than any. Her mother and father had made their
way to Rheims for the great event, and their eyes were proud and wondering. Durand Lassois was there too. And there were others.

The next day, Sunday, July 17, 1429, at nine on a fine, sunny morning, the procession began. The Dauphin glittered in his gold-encrusted
robes. He was surrounded by nobles looking almost as splendid. But

nearer to the Dauphin than any of them was Joan, splendid herself in a rich, new cloak.

Through the crowded streets they rode to the Cathedral. The huge arches of its entrance, a maze of lacy stonework, yawned to receive them. A dozen heralds blew their trumpets. Then they were in the cool gloom of the interior, spangled with jewels of lights from the great windows. At the altar, the Archbishop, in his own Cathedral at last, was waiting.

The Dauphin knelt before the Archbishop, and Joan stood in the place of honor at the Dauphin's right, holding her white standard before her.

69

She watched and listened with her face still, through the long, elaborate ceremony. Then, suddenly, her breath caught, and her eyes filled with tears. The Archbishop was lifting a tiny glass phial from a velvet cushion. He was removing the red silk stopper, and then, with a golden needle, he was probing inside the phial for a bit of the dried oil within. He was placing a tiny scrap of the dried oil on the head of the man who knelt before him.

But it made no difference how small the amount. It was the sacred oil of St. Rémy, the same oil which had once anointed Clovis himself the first King of France.

Joan had carried out the mission first laid upon her by the Archangel Michael, five years ago, in her father's garden.

The Dauphin was Dauphin no longer. He was Charles the Seventh, true King and ruler of the realm, one of the long and great procession of France's kings.

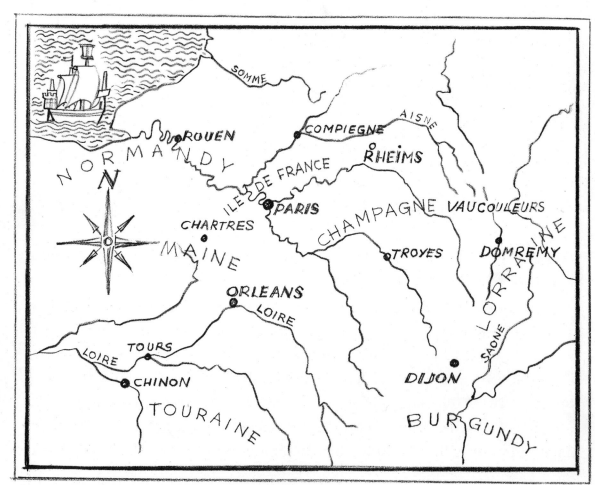

"And they told me

it must happen so . . ."

Now, in that summer, all sorts of legends began to spring up about Joan. People told each other that swarms of butterflies flew before her standard, that flocks of little birds perched in bushes to watch her passing by, that dead babies yawned and came to life when she knelt over them. These were the stories of the French, who loved her.

The English had their own legends. They told each other this terrible French girl was a witch. How else could they explain the strange daze that so often fell upon their soldiers when Joan appeared? She laid a spell upon them, that was all.

But all the while Joan grew more miraculous to others, to Joan herself it was as though the clear fire which had burned in her so long was dimmed a little, for the first time.

Perhaps she was tired. She had reason to be.

Perhaps she was homesick for the quiet of Domremy.

Or perhaps, just perhaps, deep in her heart she was beginning to really see the King for whom she had dared so much. Oh, she never showed by any word or act that this might be so. But how could she help but feel some discouragement now?

Charles the Seventh was crowned and anointed, but he was still the same hesitating, blinking fellow he had always been. He was even worse for a while, actually. Deep in *his* heart was he jealous of this girl who was so much braver and surer than he?

Joan had wanted to march with the army in an attack on Paris, immediately after the coronation. It was the next logical step in any plan to drive the English out of France.

"Well, now, let us think about this awhile," fretted Charles the Seventh. "Perhaps there is some way to get Paris without fighting."

La Trémoïlle and the Archbishop were happy to encourage Charles in this kind of thinking. They were pleased when he sent envoys to the Duke of Burgundy to arrange a truce, delighted when the Duke agreed to use his influence with the English to arrange that Paris be delivered to the King without an attack.

Only Joan seemed to realize it was just a ruse. "You will never get Paris this way," she told Charles sharply. "You will only win it at a lance's point."

Soon enough it was plain that Joan was right. The Duke of Burgundy's alliance with the English had not wavered. He sent word to the Duke of Bedford in Paris to use the time of truce for fortifying the city.

Charles only blinked when he heard this news. These days he was leading the army in an idling march from town to town, enjoying the acclaim these towns were giving him now he was King.

Beauvais was one of those cities. Its Bishop, a man named Cauchon, was so loyal to the English he thought it best to flee for his life when Charles's army approached. Hearing of his flight, did Joan's voices give her any warning that she would hear more of this man? Nobody knows, but there were those who knew that her voices had given her another sort of warning.

One day Joan was talking with her *"beau duc."* "I cannot delay like this," she said suddenly. "I dare not. I only have a year to accomplish what must be accomplished."

"What do you mean—only a year?" asked d'Alençon sharply. "What will happen to you at the end of a year?"

"I do not know," said Joan. "Perhaps I will return home to my parents. My voices just say—there is only a year."

72

D'Alençon looked at her uneasily. After that, he too began pressing the King to some kind of direct action.

Instead, Charles had a still more perverse idea. Compiègne was another city which had joyfully acclaimed him as King. Now Charles sent word to the Duke of Burgundy that he would give him the city of Compiègne, if the Duke would try again to arrange for the surrender of Paris.

Shocked and horrified, the citizens of Compiègne absolutely refused to be handed over to the Burgundians in such a fashion. But, even with Joan's startled gaze questioning him, Charles refused to be ashamed.

Still Joan was ready to fight for him as passionately as ever.

The Duke of Bedford led forth some of the English forces to confront the French. Then when his army was firmly entrenched he refused to sally out. Boldly, Joan herself rode up to the English ramparts and challenged them. But the English seemed to have caught some of Charles's own hesitation. After a few skirmishes, they withdrew and marched back to Paris.

Oh, it was a summer of endless frustration. Finally, at the end of August, Joan could stand it no longer. With very little trouble she convinced the Duke d'Alençon that the two of them, with a few men-at-arms, should ride forth to the Abbey of St. Denis, only a few miles from Paris.

The tombs of the French kings were there, it was a sacred place, but more than that, they could easily ride from there to the outskirts of Paris.

So they rode forth. Then when Joan and the Duke had studied the walls and gates and fortifications of Paris, the Duke rode back to urge the King to come toward Paris with the army. Once, twice, three times, d'Alençon made the journey, prodding the reluctant King. Finally, shaking his head and complaining, Charles the Seventh arrived with the army.

By now, of course, Paris had had weeks to prepare itself. Joan herself was not sure the time was right for an attack. But, though she prayed earnestly to her voices, they would not answer yes or no.

Joan was troubled, but her *"beau duc"* was full of eagerness and fire. Joan stood by her horse and gazed at him, her gallant friend, then she smiled and cried, "Yes—forward!"

So the French flung themselves against the ramparts of Paris, and Joan was everywhere, as always, urging the men across the moats and up the walls. All that day the struggle went on, the Parisians fighting as fiercely as their English rulers, for they had been told that Charles and the Maid would kill them all if they won the city.

It was dusk and no real progress had been made. Joan leaped into the great moat, her banner in her hand, and was wounded in the thigh by a crossbow bolt.

Even so, she would have gone on, but the Duke d'Alençon insisted that the army halt for the night. The next morning, in spite of her wound, Joan was first in the field again.

Then came two captains, riding posthaste from the King, with orders to Joan and the Duke to return at once to St. Denis.

Joan and d'Alençon looked at each other with still, set faces, then d'Alençon rode off to cancel the orders for attack. Their King had commanded. They had to obey.

Still d'Alençon had not given up. As they rode with the army toward St. Denis, d'Alençon told Joan of a bridge he had ordered built across the Seine near there. "We can cross the river up here," he said, "and ride down and attack Paris from the other side. It may be even better." Joan's heart lifted with hope, and with gratitude to her unfailing friend.

Then, as they came near St. Denis, d'Alençon reined in his horse, gave a choked cry, and pointed to the river. Joan looked. There were only the ruins of a bridge.

Later, they found out Charles himself had ordered the bridge destroyed.

Why did Charles do such things?

"Why?" cried d'Alençon. But Joan only sat quietly, staring down at the ring on her finger, and refused to ask.

But it was at St. Denis that she took off the armor she had worn at Orléans, and hung it in the chapel there, and dedicated it to the Saint, because "St. Denis is the fighting cry of France."

Then she followed the King and his army as they marched southward, away from Paris, down toward the Loire. As they came near the river, d'Alençon parted with them to go to his home in Gien for a while. Joan said good-by with tears in her eyes, though she was sure they would meet again soon.

At last they came to that restful country beyond the Loire where Charles was sure nothing could trouble him.

But Joan was not through with fighting, nor did Charles want her to be, when he discovered that some of the towns on his beloved Loire were still held by the English.

He sent Joan out with troops to win back two of those towns. The first she won easily, inspiring her soldiers in the same way she had always done. But when she came to the other, winter was closing in. The King sent her few supplies and her force was too small. At this town she knew her first real defeat.

She went back to the court then, for the winter. As the endless days dragged by she made a bitter discovery. Her *"beau duc"* had written to the King, asking to lead a force into Normandy, with Joan at his side. The King had refused him. La Trémoïlle and the Archbishop had decided that Joan and the Duke must never fight together again. Together they were too dangerous, and the Duke might soon threaten their own power.

Then the King, ashamed, perhaps, for all the ways he had failed Joan, tried to show her that in his own way, he was grateful. He enobled her and her whole family.

Joan's brothers evidently found some pleasure in this. They took the name Du Lys from the lilies on Joan's banner. But Joan kept her old name and hardly thought about the matter. Her thoughts were with the English, still in Paris, still in Normandy, and the Frenchmen who were fighting them.

75

Finally, in March, when the snows were melting, Joan broke away. In the north, the French were fighting with a contingent of their old allies, the Scotch, at their side. By Eastertime, Joan, d'Aulon, Brother Pasquerel, and a few others were in a city called Melun, south of Paris.

It was in Melun, at Eastertime, just a year after she had ridden forth to rescue Orléans, that Joan's voices gave her another warning. "Soon," they said, "you will be taken captive."

She had known that she only had a year to work for France. But somehow, being young, and always full of hope, she had never thought of capture. It chilled her heart, and she prayed and begged her voices to tell her where and when it would happen.

But her voices would not say.

There was nothing to do but go out as always, whenever, wherever France needed her.

Word came that Compiègne, that loyal city which its own King had tried to give away, was being attacked by a combined force of English and Burgundians.

Swiftly Joan gathered a group of soldiers and set forth to the rescue of Compiègne. They came toward the city through the forest behind it, riding all through one moonless night to arrive at dawn.

Joan talked with the governor of the city about its defenses, rested a while, and then, in the afternoon, she and her men rode out of the gates for a sally.

Like Orléans, Compiègne was on a river. A drawbridge spanned the river, and on the far bank was a small enemy garrison. All Joan planned

for this first sally was a quick dash against the garrison to disperse its forces up or down the river.

At first, everything went according to plan. The English were so surprised that they fled from the sight of Joan's banner as though from an oncoming storm.

Then Joan and her forces were sighted by another enemy group on the heights above the garrison. Quickly, these Englishmen sent a rider to fetch reinforcements from a Burgundian camp up the river, then they themselves joined the forces below.

Joan and her men were still undaunted. Three times they charged the increased forces, and seemed about to rout them all, when the Burgundians came galloping in from up the river.

Joan's forces were now badly outnumbered. Her soldiers stumbled toward her standard. "We must go back!" they cried. "Back—or we are lost."

"Never!" Joan shouted at them. "Only hold firm, and it is they who are lost."

But for once her men would not heed her. They were running toward the drawbridge. Joan galloped swiftly to protect their retreat as they poured onto the bridge and across it to safety. Right and left she swung with the flat of her sword, knocking down Burgundians like ninepins.

All at once there was a cry from d'Aulon, still at her side, and another from her brother, Pierre. "Look! The drawbridge!" "The gates!"

Joan looked. The drawbridge was rising. The gates to the city were closed. Either the governor had not known she was still in the field, or he had not dared wait any longer. All hope of retreat to the city was gone.

Now the English and the Burgundians saw what had happened too. For a moment they stared, then, from everywhere, they began to ride toward Joan.

Desperately, Joan spurred her horse and swung with her sword, but still only with the flat of the blade. She had never yet used it for killing. She would not use it so now.

She had managed to reach the meadow beyond the garrison when her pursuers caught up with her. All around her rose the cry, "Yield to me!" "No, no, to me!"

It was a Burgundian archer who finally grabbed the reins of her horse, and then had his hands on Joan herself, dragging her down from her horse and onto the field.

Joan the Maid had come to the end of her year.

"Take it all cheerfully

... answer boldly."

Sᴴᴇ ꜱᴛɪʟʟ ᴡᴀꜱ ɴᴏᴛ ʀᴇᴀʟʟʏ ꜰʀɪɢʜᴛᴇɴᴇᴅ. ꜱʜᴇ ᴡᴀꜱ ᴀ ᴘʀɪꜱᴏɴᴇʀ, ᴀꜱ ʜᴇʀ voices had foretold she would be. But, locked up as she was, those voices still came to her, comforting her and encouraging her. "God will help you," they said. "Take it all in good heart."

She was in a castle at first, a castle which belonged to a certain Jean de Luxembourg, master of the Burgundian archer who had taken her. D'Aulon was still with her, angry at the governor of Compiègne, whom he felt had betrayed her, and anxious about Joan's fate now.

Joan herself knew that she was a prize to her captors. She was not surprised when the Duke of Burgundy himself hurried to the castle to see with his own eyes that the Maid was truly a prisoner at last.

Still, she could hardly have guessed how thoroughly she was trapped, because she did not really know how many people she had frightened. The Burgundians hated and feared her, that she knew. And the English did too. She could easily have guessed that soon there would be dickering between those two allies as to which should have her.

But how could she have guessed, she who was in daily conversation with God's own Saints, that the Church itself hated and feared her? Oh, not every cleric and clergyman, by any means. But there was the one-time Bishop of Beauvais, Cauchon by name, who saw the Maid threatening all his hard-won career in English-held France, with her victories for Charles. There were all the theologians of the University of Paris, whose hopes were also pinned to English successes. And there were others.

Now, as the turmoil grew as to who should have her, the Burgundians, the English, or the Church, Jean de Luxembourg transferred her to another castle called Beaurevoir. D'Aulon was left behind, but the ladies of her captor's family watched over her, and, because they were kind and gentle women, Joan's life was still not really hard.

It was enough for de Luxembourg's old aunt to look into Joan's dark eyes to know this girl was good, no matter what men said. She pled with her nephew to refuse the English gold he was being offered. And she begged Joan to take on woman's clothing now.

But Joan could not consent to put aside her boy's dress. To her it seemed that would be like admitting her mission was over. And how could it be finished while the English were still thick in France, still in Paris, still besieging Compiègne?

It was the news of Compiègne's sufferings that bothered Joan most. She had failed the men and women there who looked to her for help. She walked along the battlement of the high tower where she was lodged, and her old impatience was on her. Her hands twisted together, feeling for the little ring that was no longer there. The Burgundians had taken it, along with her banner. Then she knelt and asked her Saints if there were not some way she could go to the aid of Compiègne.

"No," they said. "God will help Compiègne, but you cannot go."

Day followed day, and she grew distracted. She went to the edge of the battlement and looked down. It was a dizzying drop to the ground, sixty or seventy feet. But if there were no other way?

"Please?" she whispered to her Saints, imploring them to hold her up if she jumped.

"No," they answered. "No."

Then, for the first time in her life, she disobeyed her voices. She leaped up on the wall, looked once toward Heaven, and then jumped— out into the sheer air for that endless drop.

80   It was a miracle she was not killed. Everyone said so at the time. Men still marvel at how anyone could fall such a distance and not even break one bone. Perhaps her Saints did help her.

But she was stunned, and, after they had carried her back to her tower, she lay in a stupor for three days. Then, weeping and on her knees, she asked forgiveness of her Saints.

So the weeks of her imprisonment dragged on, and in all that while there was no word from those who were her friends.

There was no word from Charles the Seventh, no hint that he was trying to ransom her. To us, looking back, it seems incredible that he made no move to save the girl who had done so much for him. But to Joan herself perhaps it was not such a surprise. She loved her King, but she knew him too.

Still, there was her "*beau duc,*" d'Alençon. Where was he? Where was the brave Dunois of Orléans? Where were all the bold captains who had ridden at her side? Where, even, looking way back, were such loyal followers as Bertrand and Jean? Joan never asked. Perhaps they were working for her rescue in some way she did not know. Perhaps they themselves were in difficulties.

Then, suddenly, the argument as to who should have her was settled. After long parleying, her enemies realized it would be better far if she were a prisoner of the Church rather than a prisoner of war. If the Church were to try her and find her guilty of heresy, then—then the civilian authorities would be free to do what they wanted. Cauchon and clever politics had won.

But Joan only heard that she was going to be tried by the Church. And surely, she thought, that was better than being sold to the English. Why, the Church had already examined, her, at Poitiers, a year and a half ago.

The cold winds of November had begun to blow when the English guard arrived to take her to Rouen, where Cauchon was setting up an Inquisitional Court to try her. Joan shivered in her worn doublet, the same one she had been wearing before Compiègne. But she was still not frightened.

Then she came to Rouen.

She was thrown into a dungeon, and a chain was locked around her ankle and attached to a thick beam in the wall. To guard her night and day, there were five soldiers of the coarsest, most brutal type.

Quickly now, she began to find out that it was not much different to be tried by Cauchon than to be sold to the English, after all. For Cauchon himself was employed by the English, paid by the Duke of Bed-

81

ford, and he was carefully selecting the sixty churchmen who would examine her, making sure that all of them were terrified of the English for one reason or another.

For two long months, Joan waited in her cell as Cauchon assembled his court. They were nightmare months. Day and night, she had to fight off her guards as they taunted her and tried in every way to humiliate her. Day and night, a stream of curious, hostile visitors wandered in and out of her cell. Worse than any of this, though she was a prisoner of the Church, she was not allowed to hear Mass or see a priest to confess.

But when at last she was taken to the great room where her examiners waited to confront her, she knew she was facing a roomful of enemies, and she stiffened her back to fight.

"Swear now, by the Holy Gospels, to tell the truth about everything we shall ask you," said Cauchon.

82   Joan looked at his cold, proud face and said, "I do not know on what you may wish to question me. Perhaps you may ask me things I cannot answer."

A stir ran through the court. Her imprisonment had not humbled

her one bit. But she was not being merely stubborn. These men were enemies of her King as well as herself. She would tell them nothing that would endanger Charles or France.

And now began one of the strangest, most fantastic trials in all of history.

Day after day, Joan was brought before the examiners, and, day after day, there was the same wrangle about the oath. Then there was the questioning.

Quickly enough they covered the bare outline of her short life. They were not much interested in that anyway. It was her voices which obsessed them. What made her so sure they came from God? How did she know the names of her Saints?

At first Joan still had hopes that the examination at Poitiers would be of some help. "I have been asked about that," she would say. "Look in the book of Poitiers."

But, as Cauchon's lips closed in a thin, tight line, Joan realized that the book of Poitiers meant nothing here. Either Cauchon had destroyed it, or hidden it. It was gone.

Very well. She would answer the question if she could. But sometimes, when the questions grew too impossible, she would simply say, "*Passez outre.*" "Go on to the next."

Then they came to the business of her clothes, which seemed almost as blasphemous as her claim to have heard directly from God. Who told her to wear boy's clothes? Who, why, where, and how?

Then they were back to her Saints. Did they have hair? Did they wear crowns?

Suddenly, they were recalling the Fairy Tree from her long-ago childhood. She had danced around that tree. That meant she believed in fairies and such witchcraft, did it not?

They brought up her ring. She had blessed people with it, had she not?

Then they were back to the Saints, and the boy's dress again.

Perhaps it only seems like a senseless circle to us. We do not believe in witches any more, or in people being possessed of the Devil. We do not see how such questions, day after day, were designed to force Joan into some sort of admission that she was so possessed.

And, of course, that was not all the trial was about. These men were not simply frightened of her because she had achieved such victories over the English. They were frightened of her as churchmen. The Church on earth, the Church Militant, with all its popes, cardinals, archbishops, bishops, and priests, existed to receive and interpret God's commands. But here and there, all over Europe in these days, men were arising who said that the individual had some rights to interpret God's will for himself. To the Church Militant, this was the heresy of Protestantism. And Joan's claim was part of it. If they allowed her to maintain it, the heresy would spread.

"Do you still hear your voices?" they asked.

"Yes!" she said. "Every day. They tell me: 'Answer boldly.' They say I will receive help. 'Do not despair on account of your martyrdom,' they say. 'In the end you will come to the Kingdom of Heaven.'"

She still was not frightened. She thought her martyrdom was the pain and suffering she was undergoing in her cell and through these endless weeks of questioning.

84

Then, at last, after seven weeks of it, the examiners wrote up their findings, and then brought her back to read her their conclusions. Then she found out she had one chance, and one chance only, to save her life.

She could give up her claim that her voices came from God. She could deny them, and reject her visions too, as inventions of her own imagination.

It was impossible, of course. She told them so in court. She told them so when, in pairs or groups, they visited her cell. Then they took her to a torture chamber. They were going to give her every chance to admit her follies and embrace the Church.

"Deny your voices came from God," they said, and showed her the rack.

And suddenly she was flaming at them.

"If I were to be condemned and saw the fire lit, and the wood prepared, and the executioner who was to burn me ready to cast me into the fire, still in the fire I would not say anything other than what I have said."

Cauchon and his examiners talked it over for a moment. They decided it would be foolish to torture her. They would simply sentence her and have done with it.

There was a great gathering out-of-doors in Rouen, with Joan on one platform, and Cauchon and some of the examiners on another, and a grinning, excited mob all around.

Cauchon started to read aloud the Proclamation of Excommunication. ". . . And so you are abandoned as a limb of Satan, and severed from the Church——"

Suddenly, Joan cried out, and stretched out her arms to stop him. Her words of the day before had been too brave. She saw the wood prepared, and she was frightened, terribly, terribly frightened, of the fire.

She burst into great sobs, and, as Cauchon hurried to her with a confession to sign, her eyes were so blurred with tears she could hardly see to make the sign which stood for her signature.

She was only nineteen, after all. Bravely and boldly, she had stood all alone, day after day for months, while that great panel of hostile judges hammered at her.

They thought they had broken her spirit at last.

"Still in the fire,

I would say no different . . ."

SHE HAD RECANTED, SIGNED THE CONFESSION CAUCHON HAD PREPARED, and then listened numbly as he read the new sentence. Then she was led back to the same cold, filthy cell she had been in so long.

They gave her a woman's gown to wear and left her with the same five brutal guards.

One day, two days, three, Joan stayed there in her cell. Then, on the third day, one of the guards hurried to fetch Cauchon.

He found Joan sitting on her cot dressed in her boy's clothing. The guards knew why. They should have. They were the ones who had taken away the woman's dress and left her only the doublet and hose if she wanted to get up from her cot.

But Joan chose to ignore the guards. She said she had taken back the boy's dress of her own free will, because it seemed more suitable. And because Cauchon had not kept his promise that she should hear Mass and be relieved of her fetters.

Further, she told the Bishop that her voices had spoken to her in these days and told her that she had done great wrong to God in confessing that what she had done was not well done.

"I never intended to deny my Saints," she said. "It was fear of the fire that made me do it." Her voice was steady, and she gazed into Cauchon's eyes, knowing exactly what she was saying.

It was what he really had hoped for all along, what the English hoped for too, much better than a confession. She had confessed and then re-lapsed into sin. There was no question about her excommunication now, and then the civil authorities could take over.

There were just a few formalities first. Then, on Wednesday, May 30, 1431, Cauchon sent a priest to Joan's cell so that she might receive Communion. It was against all churchly law for a relapsed person to receive Communion. Deep in his heart was Cauchon beginning to feel uneasiness and shame?

86

Then the guards took Joan out into the market place, where soldiers and townspeople had gathered in a great crowd. There was a platform for the judges, another for the priests, and one which simply held a stake, piled round with wood.

They led her first to the priests, who read out the proclamation that she was a relapsed heretic. She knelt and wept and prayed forgiveness for herself and everybody.

Not all the priests were without feeling. There were those standing there who were sick with shame, and they could not look at Joan. But it was an English soldier who fashioned a rude cross out of two sticks and handed it to her as she rose from her knees.

Then they led her from that platform to the other, and put a paper cap on her head, bearing the words "Heretic! Apostate!"

Then they bound her to the stake and piled the wood around her. One priest stood on the platform holding a crucifix. Joan called to him to get down before the fire was lighted, but still to hold the cross high.

Then the wood was lighted and the flames leaped up. And in the terrible hush that fell over the market place everyone heard Joan call out to her Saints. "St. Catherine! St. Margaret! St. Michael!"

The flames were a torch. They hid her from view. Only her high, sweet voice that had floated over so many battlefields floated out now from the fire, as she called out the name on her ring—the name on her standard—the name on her heart—"Jesus!"

So she died. And even that day, in the sick reaction that so often follows such a deed, an Englishman cried out, "We are lost. We have burned a Saint."

They *were* lost. The vision of unity that Joan had given to the people of France did not die with her. Instead, it grew ever stronger. Finally, thirty years later, in 1461, every English invader had left French soil.

In those years, Joan's poor hesitating King managed to stiffen his backbone a bit too. He got rid of his two poor advisors, and found better and wiser ones. And finally, in his own delaying, backhanded way, he even came to Joan's rescue, ordering the Church to hold a new trial and clear her of the charge of heresy.

And, of course, as everyone knows, the Church has long since gone further than that in overruling those poor, driven churchmen at Rouen. In this very century, Joan was canonized as a Saint.

Still, nobody says you have to believe in her voices. Believe what *you* have to believe, as she did. For her voices were not the most astonishing thing about her anyway. The astonishing thing is the *way* she believed in them, even unto death, and everything else that she did—so young, and so alone.

88

A.D.
1431